DATE DUE

NOV 0 5 2012	
MAY 0 9 2013	
FEB 0 4 20??	
FEB 05 2015	
JUN 1 4 2018	
MAR 1 4 2019	

I Use
Science Tools

by Kelli Hicks

Science Content Editor:
Kristi Lew

www.rourkepublishing.com

Science content editor: Kristi Lew

A former high school teacher with a background in biochemistry and more than 10 years of experience in cytogenetic laboratories, Kristi Lew specializes in taking complex scientific information and making it fun and interesting for scientists and non-scientists alike. She is the author of more than 20 science books for children and teachers.

www.rourkepublishing.com

Photo credits:
Cover © sevenke, Cover logo frog © Eric Pohl, test tube © Sergey Lazarev; Page 3 © Chamille White; Page 5 © ZouZou; Page 7 © sevenke; Page 9 © Rob Marmion; Page 11 © auremar; Page 13 © Ammit; Page 15 © Tracy Whiteside; Page 17 © tonobalaguerf; Page 19 © bendao; Page 20 © Rob Marmion; Page 22 © tonobalaguerf, sevenke, Rob Marmion; Page 23 © auremar, Tracy Whiteside, bendao

Editor: Jeanne Sturm

Cover and page design by Nicola Stratford, bdpublishing.com

Library of Congress Cataloging-in-Publication Data

Hicks, Kelli L.
 I use science tools / Kelli Hicks.
    p. cm. -- (My science library)
Includes bibliographical references and index.
ISBN 978-1-61741-729-0 (Hard cover)
ISBN 978-1-61741-931-7 (Soft cover)
1. Scientific apparatus and instruments--Juvenile literature. I. Title.
Q185.3.H53 2011
502.8'4--dc22
                          2011003759

Rourke Publishing
Printed in the United States of America,
North Mankato, Minnesota
060711
060711CL

www.rourkepublishing.com - rourke@rourkepublishing.com
Post Office Box 643328 Vero Beach, Florida 32964

Are you ready to use science tools in the science lab?

As you work, use a pencil to write down what you learn.

A **hand lens** makes small things look bigger.

If it is very tiny, use a **microscope** to look at it.

A camera takes pictures of what you see.

Use a **ruler** to measure how long something is.

A **scale** shows how much something weighs.

CAPACITY 5kg
SENSITIVITY 20g

15

Measure liquid in
a **beaker.**

A **timer** counts down time.

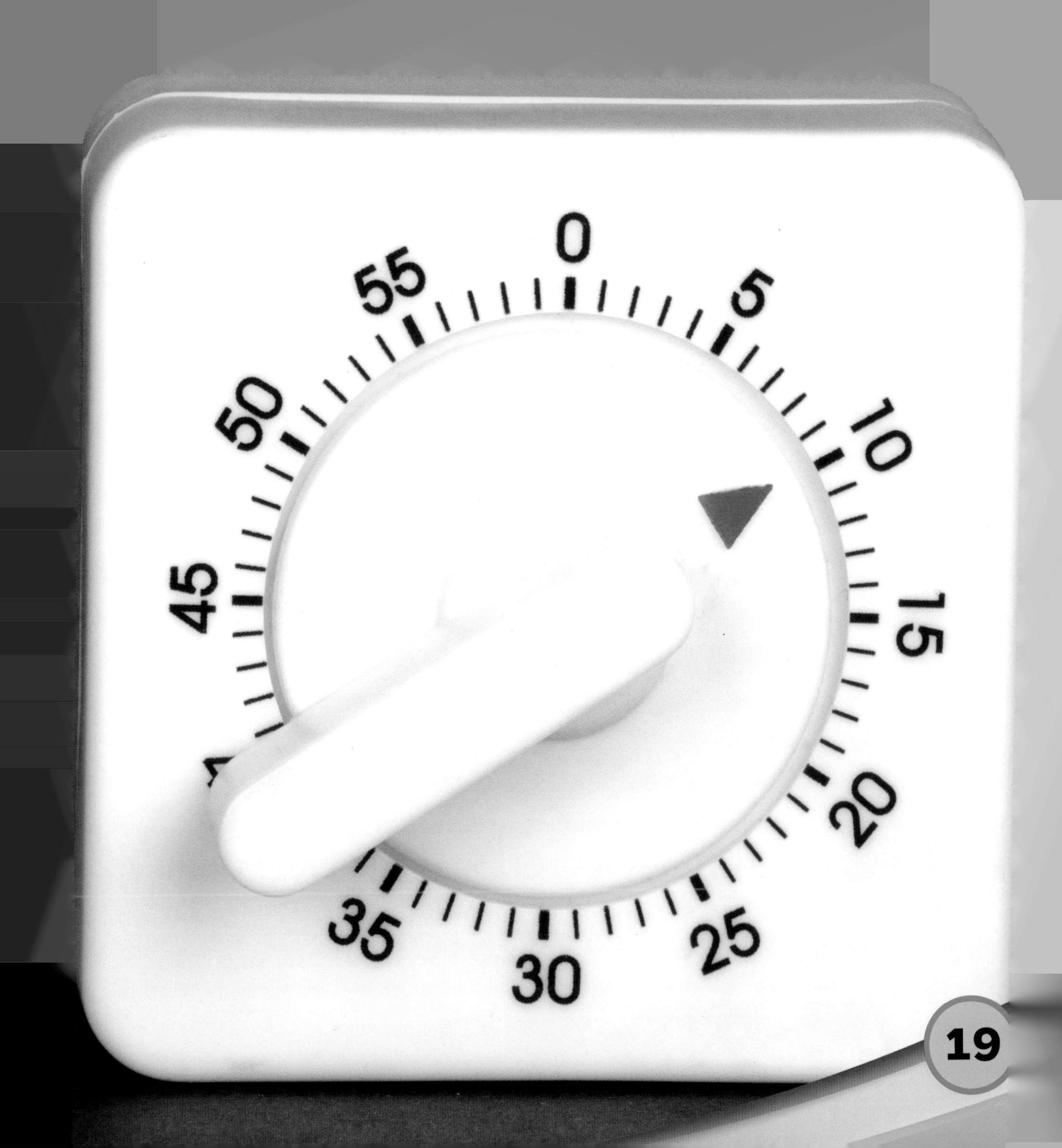
0
5
10
15
20
25
30
35
45
50
55

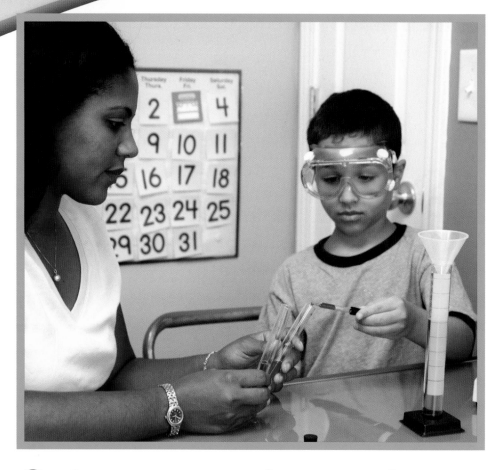

Science tools make
the work easier.

SHOW what you know

1. How do tools help you in science?

2. Why would you need to use a microscope?

3. If you were a scientist, what tools would you need?

Picture Glossary

beaker (BEE-kur):
A beaker is a plastic or glass jar with a spout for measuring and pouring liquids.

hand lens (HAND lenz):
This is a glass lens that you hold in your hand. It makes things look bigger.

microscope (MYE-kruh-skope):
A microscope has powerful lenses that make small things look bigger.

ruler (ROO-lur):
A ruler is a long, flat piece of wood, plastic, or metal that you use for measuring distance.

scale (SKALE):
A scale is a tool used for weighing things.

timer (TIME-ur):
A timer is a tool that counts down an amount of time. Timers ring when the time is up.

Index

Websites

www.sciencemadesimple.com

http://school.discoveryeducation.com

http://scifun.chem.wisc.edu

About the Author

Kelli Hicks loves to write books for kids. She loves to learn about science and nature. She uses tools to fix things in her house and to work in the yard. She lives in Tampa with her husband, her kids Mackenzie and Barrett, and their golden retriever, Gingerbread.